MORIVIVÍ
To Have Died
yet Lived

MORIVIVÍ
To Have Died
yet Lived

Kamilah Mercedes Valentín Díaz

ALEGRIA
PUBLISHING

Library of Congress Control number: 9798986084435
ISBN: 979-8-9860844-3-5

Published by Alegria Publishing
Book cover and layout by Carlos Mendoza

Morivivi: To have Died yet Lived

For me
and you.

Us.

If you have nothing to hold onto
hold onto this book.

Grasp it tightly in your hands,
so that the pages begin to crease
and your fingers start to go numb.

Read it; when you're ready.

Just exist in this moment
for a second, a minute, an hour, a day.
Take as long as you need.

I promise that it will all be worth it.

Table of Contents

Foreword
Written by Gabriela Valentin Diaz

Morivivís grow wildly in our grandparents' yards in Puerto Rico. They open up towards the sun and close quickly to the touch. Morivivís are also known by other names like vergonzosa and dormilona. They are an apt representation for Kamilah's intense journey - to go from reveling freely in the sun, to sinking within yourself, closed off to the outside. *Morivivi: To have Died yet Lived* immerses you in Kamilah's thoughts through the most difficult point of her life. It is an introspective collection that shares her pain, but also her will to live a full, authentic life.

As the oldest of las nenas, it has been my privilege and duty to witness Kamilah's discovery of herself as a writer and poet. She has had a penchant for words since she was a child, however, in the summer of 2021 when she began her treatment for depression, I saw and heard a new tempo to her thoughts. Kamilah was suddenly calling to enthusiastically describe her ideas for her writings in detail. Novels, poems, screenplays; I could listen to her talk for hours. It was the first time in a long time you could hear excitement in her voice. She began performing her poetry for us.

Her words, especially those she wrote with the intention of sharing them, carried a deeper understanding of her perspective and voice as a writer. It was like Kamilah's mind had unlocked a new plane, reserved for her words and ideas. Kamilah was broken, yet she filled the space created by her brokenness with her art. I often wonder if Kamilah would have realized that she is and always has been a writer without her mental health journey. While this question will remain unanswered, what I do know is that her art is one of the reasons she is here today. And for that we are grateful.

To see Kamilah Mercedes Valentín Díaz through our eyes is a gift. To hear her words and intimately know the fire that fuels them is a divine experience. This is what you will get from Morivivi. This collection shows you the sharpest corners of Kamilah's soul, but also her fighting spirit and the soft yet fierce love she has for our island, people, and most recently, herself.

As you navigate through the peaks and valleys of Kamilah's life through her poetry, my hope is that this collection is a place of solace for those who can connect with Kamilah's feelings and experience. At the very least, this collection will help you understand at least a fraction of the pride that I feel for my little sister.

A nuestra Kamy, our chispo: gracias por nunca dejar de compartir tu corazón tan libremente con nosotros. Te amamos, bebé.

Preface

I never understood people who said they never thought about how they would die. I used to think about my death all the time. How I hoped it wasn't embarrassing or abrupt, and I knew I didn't want to die by fire or drowning. I never thought I would die by suicide, let alone contemplate it, but I suppose that's life. We never know the turns it will take.

It wasn't until February 2020, during the pandemic, that I realized I was severely depressed. And though I didn't want to die, I felt deeply in my core that the only way this new experience I found myself struggling with would end would be in my death. Everyday I would wake and wait until I could go back to sleep because it was in sleep I could find a semblance of solace, quiet. Every night I went to sleep I wondered if I would wake up again.

I did.

I began writing as a means of processing what I was experiencing, and a way to cope with all the noise going on inside my head. The opportunity presented itself for me to join a writing community and publish a book. I leapt at it. Every day it felt like I was poised on death's door, so might as well try and chase your dreams before you're gone. It became a lifeline. As I continued writing, I thought of many titles for my first collection. None of them satisfied me. Until I landed on one that encapsulated my exact situation, *Morivivi: To have Died yet Lived.*

A morivivi is an actual thing, not a made up word. A morivivi is a plant which I became familiar with because it grows on mi islita del encanto. When touched it closes its leaves. Retracting into itself for protection. It also reacts in the same way at dusk. Like many Boricuas, growing up I would play with the morivivi, testing its instincts, and fascinated by its reflexes. I wonder if it ever got tired. I hope someone let it rest.

Much like the morivivi, I found myself closing up, retracting, and feeling unsafe 24/7. I was always on edge, and I feared (among a lot of other things) that I would never open up again. It seemed impossible. It felt all-consuming. I didn't start opening up by chance. I had my family which I love wholeheartedly, and I am extremely lucky that they love me back. I had access to therapy. I had art. I had physical health. I had Puerto Rico.

I think it's possible to die while you're alive. That's the only way I can describe what I went through. Morí. Viví. I died, yet I lived.

In this bilingual collection, Morivi: To have Died yet Lived, I want to share with my readers my shame, my hurt, my heart, and my hope. I want you to feel held and comforted. I want people to know that it's okay if you have to close up, so long as you remember to try and open up again.

Try again.

That's all I ask.

"Lucha que lucha,
no podrán llevarme a la tumba."

You Die more than Once

I didn't want to die. I wanted to look inside
myself and not pale
at what I saw.

I didn't want to die.
I wanted to yearn
again.

I scrambled for a way to halt
the weapons of mutually assured destruction
firing across my synapses. But, fear

became a faithful friend.

Like an unfurling wave my hands
did little to fend off the crash
of incoming darkness. Like Kronos, I imagined myself the villain
rightfully cast away to the inescapable depths of Tartarus.

I made myself judge, jury, and ex-I didn't
want to die. I wanted
this feeling to stop.

If little deaths
were meant to be pleasant
then this was a big one.

(S)pain

Intrusive yet elusive.
A wisp in the psyche.
Buy a ticket for a bullet-

train.
Destination, (S)pain.

Stranger's Eyes

I saw a stranger in the mirror today.
A wailing woman with a haunted look
embedded beneath her shadowed eyes.

Her lips attempted to shape the words,
I love you, but they disintegrated.
They never got past her chapped lips.

When I realized she was me, I shied away.
I wasn't ready

to peer into what her expression foretold
to pilfer through what emotions were waiting in store.

In Circles

I feel so on edge.
Almost like I'm running for that ledge.
I must wait 'til I reach the end
before I make my peace and take that leap at the bend.

I feel so on edge.
All these thoughts tumbling round up my head.
Round round round they go. Just outside my reach
and then they're no more.

Treading Water

This feeling
it's like swimming towards shore
and hoping you don't run out of air
before you feel dry sand between your toes.

Ears ringing,
head underwater,
and pitch black.

The current pushes you back
and you have to start again.
Never quite sure of the progress you've made.

Dropped in the middle of the ocean without a life jacket.
An anchor tied to your ankle pulling you deeper
left to wonder if it's best to let the water in.

Bubbles escape your nose and mouth. Escaping
the way you wish you could.

Aprueba de Fuego

Mi piel de hierro

vencerá tus llamas.

I am Kindling

While I stood in the flames burning
I realized it was a fire of my own making.
An amateur arsonist.
I struck the first match,

and fed fuel to a rage outside of my domain.
The time I spent feeling the burn began to blur
until I was ready to control the blaze on my own.

The smoke I inhaled was no longer tinged by melancholy
flames they provided the warmth of a candle
with the force of an inferno, and the promise of heat
kept the monsters at bay.

False Teeth

Wear your smiles, don't let them wear you
out. The forced smile is the heaviest

to carry, and the hardest to muster.
A smile isn't a fashion accessory

though it is often treated as one. A genuine smile has the power
to fill you, motivate you.

To smile or not to smile
that is the question.

Whichever you choose, let it express the truth that lies within.
Not the veneer you wish to project upon the world.

Forsaken Silence

What do you do
when at your core you crave
the deepest of connections,
but dread that your essence drips
poison from a red-painted lip?

What do you do
when silence shatters glass
on a high note?

Before silence screamed
your eyes held a gleam.
Now they hold a message
you can't quite glean.

Spider Silk in the Attic

My words were swept
away by a sea-grass woven broom.

Dust pan at the ready
to collect cobwebs crowding
the blank space nestled
between my ears.

Winter Sucks

I'm left parched
like when I was little
and drank too much Sunny D.

Lips permanently pursed
and a bitter taste stuck
to the roof of my mouth.

My tongue feels funny.

The biting cold
nips at my fingertips.
So sharp it draws blood
to the surface of my skin.

Leeching the warmth out
from underneath.
Revealing my undertones
of ghastly green.

Snow clouds my glasses.
Tiny wind-sheild wipers.
An idea for a patent.

Winter sucks me dry. A beautiful torment.
I call it the vampire season for a reason, but

if I slip and fall
know it wasn't my fault.

No Disco, all Inferno

Turn the handle.

The water?
Scalding.

It helps drive out the cold.

Step in,

with the intention of standing
only to end up on the floor.

Body curled inward, over my knees,
imitating the steam
caressing my neck.

Deep breaths
echo in time
with the pulse
of the showerhead.

The rushing water paints my hair to my skull
baptizing me in sorrow
as I cleanse myself
to face another tomorrow.

Open Wounds

If you have to cry,
cry
a river's worth of tears.

If you wanna scream,
scream
as loud as you can.

Let it out.
Let it hurt.
Let it breathe.

And when you're done,
keep going.

It's not like shedding a coat

It's not pretty;
it's exhausting
and uninviting.

A snake
molting.

A lizard
regenerating its tail.

It's brutal.
It's real.

I wasn't born to be easy
or simple that much I've gathered.

My time? It's now
and it's only as good
as I allow it to be.

This present is a gift
I give to myself.

I am learning to accept who I was,
who I am, and who I wish to be.

As I shed my old self
and mold a new horizon,

I'm sure it won't be the last time
I'll have to start from scratch.

Water Thyself

I was a garden left unattended.
Weeds and parasites overran my flower bed.
Not a caretaker in sight
to water me, nourish me.

I realized if I waited around
growth would allude me.

I learned to tend to myself and lean into the sun.
To bloom with intention and go with the flow.

I learned to turn over fresh soil and leave room
for new things to take root.

Water thyself, I said.
Replenish your reservoirs. A smidge of Miracle-Gro
could turn out to be a miracle worker.
Let the water douse you and quench your thirst.

Water thyself, I said.
The water knows
where it needs to go.
The water knows, and it does not judge.

It Starts with a Chorus

The history of the White Man seeks to erase
the stories and culture
of those they failed to exterminate

dance in the wind carried by words spoken
in soft reverent tones.

The White Man would rip tongues
from the root
of those who dared
share their tales.

Stories spread with the quickness of wildflowers
and the ferocity of wildfires,
once let loose
they become difficult to tame.

Give thanks
to that flowering flame,

and let the world sing
the words denied to them for centuries.

May we hear the voices
of our ancestors ring
true like cathedral stained
glass.

Oleaje

Mi angustia, como la marea, va y viene en olas.
Me arrastra de un punto a otro a máxima velocidad.

No se sabe dónde empieza ni dónde termina.
El principio y el final. Unidos representan lo que es
y lo que un día será.

El océano nació sin merced para nadie.
Todo regresa a su estabilidad cósmica.

No te preocupes; ocúpate.
No te inquietes buceando por la calma que llegará

en su momento.
Al compás del mar.

Mi Luz

La casa de mi bisabuela
quedaba al frente de una calle
como cualquier otra. Las casas enfila'
como cuando ponen una finca a producir.

En casa de mi bisabuela
había un palo de aguacate en el patio
y tenían un cuadro de un payaso
espantoso guindao' en el pasillo.

En casa de mi bisabuela
fue donde yo tuve mi primera experiencia
con la serenidad. La receta secreta
era arroz blanco con salchichas de lata y kétchup.

En casa de mi bisabuela
yo era la picúa y el chispo
a la que le decían,
        - Esa nena tiene los rizos tan bonitos.
En casa de mi bisabuela
me daban pesetas enrolla' en papel toalla
a escondidas con el mensajito:
        - No dejes que nadie lo vea.

En casa de mi bisabuela
yo corría detrás de los lagartijos.
Jamás cache uno pero a veces me quedaba con la cola
sin querer.

En casa de mi bisabuela
nos sentábamos en el balcón
a contar los carros a lo que pasaban.
2 rojos, 4 azules, 6 blancos.

En casa de mi bisabuela
catalogué unas memorias claras de mi niñez.
Por primera vez sentí la fuerza del amor antiguo
sin complicaciones y lleno de sabiduría.

En mi memoria, la casa de mi bisabuela permanece
como un faro en la distancia.
Alumbrándome el camino
con su luz eterna.

Shadows Lurking

He comes up behind me when I least expect it
his steps shadowing me and I never see
it coming until it's too late.

His eyes are beady and filled with malice.
His hair is lanky and level with his brows.

Nose upturned, and lips pulled back
as he prepares to snarl diatribes my way.

He doesn't know why,
but he hates me.

He doesn't know my name, where I'm from,
who I love, or who loves me.

He knows that I don't look like him
and that's enough.
His great-great-great grandfather fought in some war
and he gazes at me as if I were the one across enemy lines.

He believes girls are fragile, stupid, and dramatic.
Except for the brown ones, those are dangerous,
angry, spicy; his Daddy said so.

He's the rent-a-cop that threatened to shoot
if we didn't turn the car around.

I learned to not cower
from him. I have nothing to be ashamed of.

I'll never apologize for who I am, and yet I pity him
because he knows nothing.

He doesn't know that there are other paths. He was blinded
before he knew how to spell his own name. He can keep hating me
until his face starts to wrinkle and his hair thins away.

While he does that, I'll be busy
living as my memory of him fades into shades of gray.

Who knows,

maybe he's you?

Break Fast

You tapped me persistently on the edge
of a countertop, cracked

me open like an egg
with its yolk broken.

Discarded, my milky-white shell
lies empty.

Cuadros Vacios

Hay gente que con una sola mirada
puede hacerte sentir
como si estuvieras pintado en la puta pared.

Pero lo que no reconocemos
es que esa frase le da poder al enemigo.

Los que te menosprecian
no merecen el respeto, el mérito, ni el crédito
que se les da a los artistas.

Al contrario, ellos no crean solo destruyen.
Esos quienes tienen mentes creativas superan
a ellos que las tienen vacías.

Intentan llenar ese hueco con malicia
y cuando no pueden marcan a los demás en su travesía.

Lo único que forra sus paredes son cuadros vacíos
que enmarcan lo que podría haber sido.

La Revolución Vive en Mí

Borinquen bella, I may leave
your shores, but you will never leave me.

You are what my bones are made of. You
are in my DNA. There is no me

without you. Wherever I go, you go
because I carry pieces of you within.
It is not a heavy weight to bare,
but one I cherish. A consistent one to hold onto
on cold hard winter days.
Borinquen bella, I will rebel in your name.

Porque la revolución, vive en mí,
la llevo en mi sangre.
I will live freely and boldly. As long as I do, those pieces of you
will also know the taste of freedom.

Borinquen bella, goodbye for now,
but never forever. Always, until next time.

Society is Calling

We are unsuspecting pieces
to a game
we never learned the rules for.

Manipulated and monopolized
for eternity
with no one to bail us out.

Cantaito

En Puerto Rico, siguen cerrando escuelas.
Nos quieren complacientes
en nuestra propia destrucción.

Nos tienen con las manos esposadas
detrás de la espalda. Para que cuando nos metan la espada
no podamos sacarla.

En Puerto Rico, no nos cuentan
nuestra historia. En vez nos empujan
la gloria de Cristóbal Colón hasta que nos quedemos atragantao'.

Nos tienen encadenados
en el pasado y en el presente. Oprimidos
bajo el mando del colonialismo.

En Puerto Rico, somos un país
sometido a la dominación del capitalismo. Nos roban
del derecho a ser autosuficientes y nos vendan los ojos para no ver

como con cada corporación que invade nuestras playas
se llevan un mordisco
de nuestra patria.

Nos quieren mellados como un perro
cuyo único recurso sea ladrar.

En Puerto Rico, los americanos vienen
a darse una probadita de nuestras diversiones y naturaleza
pero le pagan al mismo gringo para darle una imitación barata de
nuestra cultura.

Nos tienen escondidos detrás de la cortina
como el mago de Oz.

En Puerto Rico, los recursos permanecen ocultos
del pueblo y los políticos se quitan la responsabilidad
de encima jugando al escondite.

Dicen,
—Cogemos de pendejo hasta los nuestros–
doblados entre carcajadas
pero como quiera hay aquellos que los apoyan
y se amparan de las consecuencias.

En Puerto Rico, pasa un huracán que deja más de 3 mil muertos
y la nación que se titula como dueño se la pasa callando
nuestros llantos.

Nos fuerzan bajo el agua
hasta que se nos corte la respiración.

En Puerto Rico, se violan los derechos humanos.
Todo por una ideología que nos impuso el conquistador blanco.

Nos importa más que dos hombres se besen
a que los niños tengan un hogar sano.

Me siento con la libertad de hablar
al calzón quitado porque amo a mi país.

Amo mi gente, amo mi cultura, amo mis playas y mis montañas,
amo mi arroz con gandules, y al señor que grita,
—Parcha, coco, piña—
sin faltar.

Canto porque le digo no más
al abuso de mi patria.

When Hunger Strikes

Those who derive their strength from the pain of others
are not powerful. They are power hungry.

Feasting on misery
instead of celebrating triumphs.
They are always hankering for more.

Indeed, power is addictive,
but what will be the result when the supply runs short?
When there is no one left to extort?

This pyramid scheme is in the midst
of collapse and the ones who once found themselves ruling oceans
will find themselves stranded on dry land.

Behind Closed Doors

I-N-S-I-D-E.
Some people say that it is what's on the inside that counts,
but things lurk
inside; dark, twisted, inexplicable things.

Would you like to come inside?
It might be fun inside.
But is it bright inside? Light inside?

I-N-S-I-D-E.
Some people say you find the truth on the inside.
Things hide
inside; dark, twisted, inexplicable things.

Will verity be found inside? Does it grant you clarity
Inside? But is it bright inside? Light inside?
Or will you find fright inside?

Collision Course

Crossing the street
I thought of jumping
in front of a moving car.

Not to play chicken
or leave it with enough time
to come to a complete stop.

The play-by-play of events flashed through my head
cued up on a *Viewmaster* my finger poised
on its yellow lever. My feet remained planted
firmly where the sidewalk met the road.

How bizarre.

The urge to comply
banging around
droning to the beat of a drum
in my hollowed out skull.

Eyes closed,
I counted the cracks
lining the cement.
I waited

until the cars passed
and made my way across.

Libertad

Me tiraron hacia el cielo
para ver si podía volar.
Pero, poco a poco,
me fueron cortando las alas.

Yo Merezco mi Paz

My valentía shows when I fight
against the worst thoughts I have about myself.
If I can stand up for myself against myself
entonces puedo con todo. I aim for more
then to continue this brega. I aim to thrive.

I aim to feel vida coursing relentlessly through my veins
with the force of oceans. To emerge reborn and able
to claim my strength. To stand in my power and bask in the glory
of my renacimiento- unafraid and sin vergüenza.

The fear and pain will have lifted
and the light filtering in
will brush up against my corazón.
Once again alight with alegria.

No longer will the night control me.
La noche será mía. I will regain my friendship
with soledad and value her for the clarity she gives me.
I will be free.

L i b r e.

My sueñito is not to rest in peace, but to live
peacefully with abandon.

I will get there porque la lucha
doesn't have a deadline.

Buscando Razones

Cuando se te van las sonrisas
y no encuentras razones
para sacar los dientes.

Cuando descubres que ya no te sale el canto tan fácil como antes.
Cuando antes tarareabas sin darte cuenta.

Cuando no le encuentras el dulce al pan
y el café se convierte en cenizas
bailando por tu paladar.

Te atragantás.

El gusto ya no es el mismo
y las cosas especiales en tu vida ahora son difíciles de soportar.

Todo te molesta.

La vida está hecha para celebrar
no tolerar.

Pero sabes que llegará un punto cuando tú mente y corazón digan,
—No más, basta.

Taínos

your blood runs through my veins
yet I question if I have any right
to that claim.

Is blood enough
or should I let this feeling wane?

I do not wish
to step on the throats
of those who came before
and are still here.

Taínos, the Spaniards came for gold
but stayed to enslave,
murder, and lay waste
to your way of life.

Taínos, you were uprooted
from your land and your culture,
but what they didn't know is that they left behind a sliver
of your soul within the soil.

And that sliver like a small and incessant flame remained
in order to set this world ablaze.
Taínos, you have been colonized multiple times
over the course of your existence.

I do not consider it a successful genocide
because you have survived. Your spirit is persistent.
The hand that guides you is unknown
to this realm we exist in.

Taínos, you are real.
I insist it. You refuse to fade
away through this passage of time.

Taínos, the passing of time has brought you out of the woodwork.
I have seen your renaissance. Hell, I am living it.

Taínos, I am proud to be among your ranks.
As I learn about my ancestors, dig deep
to stand my ground and flourish. I will help
in this cultural re-propagation.

Instead of a pot I will place you in the wilds,
so your roots may expand across this land once more.
As I learn to unabashedly claim and exclaim my heritage.

¡Yo voy a ti, Taíno!

Hand-stitched

Work with the needle,
not the hammer.

Progress is progress.
Is progress is progress.

You've got nothing to prove,
the only person you need to satisfy is you.

Little White Lies

If they're white they're granted clemency
anything but and they execute them on sight.
There's even a saying for the double-standard.

They call them little white lies
and they're always exonerated for their crimes.
The crime is white or is it right and then forgotten.

The system grins and chants,
"Everything's All White"
as the rest of us bleed and fight for our rights.

It's all move on and keep calm as they gaslight us.

Hide away their dirty laundry and hang us out to dry.
Then they have the caucasity to act surprised
when those they emboldened try to topple them on their side.

Suck on that lemon and swallow your pride
'cause it's high time we challenged the tide.

Brown Skin

In the summer I am brown
like a stick of canela
in your coquito
on Noche Buena.

In the winter I am brown
washed-out like the innards
of a mushroom's flesh
spilling out.

Arena Corriendo entre mis Manos

Las olas gritan
mi nombre. El viento acaricia
mi piel. Los árboles me sacan a bailar.
La tierra me abraza.

Poco a poco el recuerdo se va borrando.
Mientras el mundo sigue girando, mi realidad se va
desintegrando.

De grano en grano hasta que me quede deshecha.

Lo que sobran son piezas sin patrón
y el reto de volverme a montar
como el rompecabezas que nunca fui.

No hay de otra.

Que se joda el rompecabezas
y manos a la obra.

Que soy un fucking mosaico.

Unleash the Witch

I have a theory
that all women are witches.

The songs that we speak are spells
we cast. The words we scream are curses
thrown your way. Our perfumes are our potions.
And our jewels are our crystals.

Mother Nature is a woman, and what is nature
but magic expressing itself across the universe
only to emerge at a given point. That point
being the earth we currently sit on.

I have a theory
that all women are witches. They may burn us, drown us,
turn us against each other and yet,
here we are still standing despite it all.

Woman, you are incandescent. You
are a beautiful miracle.

Witch, unleash your power. Unleash yourself
upon this world.

Inky Depths

My soul is an inkpot.
I dip a quill into

its depths.
And write a story,
scribbled in chicken-scratch

illegible to me.

Self-portrait

Trust is a bust
I pushed off its pedestal.

I dodged
to not get crushed.

Better it turn to dust
before its plinth combusts.

Reassurance

You could tell me my hair is purple
even though it isn't. That shade
would soon overtake my face.

I'd beg. I'd plead.

Please confirm the truth
for me. Sometimes I fear
I cannot see
myself clearly.

Reflections

When you look in the mirror
and feel the urge to reinvent yourself

that's the voice of your courage speaking
not failure.

Treat me Gentle

Place me inside a vase.
Where it's nice, warm, and safe.
Cool porcelain pressed
up against my cheek.

I am viscous.

My body leans into the curves
of its Alchemilla-stamped space.

Reverie or Revelry?

Some of us ignore pain and suffering
because it's ugly.

Others choose to revel in it
because it's beautiful.

We have to choose between remaining ignorant
or becoming devious. Neither help
in ending this vicious cycle.

Volando

Prefiero quedarme en las nubes.
La tierra no está preparada
pa' sostenerme.

Al Sartén

Siempre me han dicho
que mi sangre es dulce
para los mosquitos. Imagino,

mi sangre fluyendo
como miel o syrup
que se le echa encima
a los pankei. Pero

también es sangre que siente
sangre que hierve. Su calor
es capaz de freir una docena
de huevos para que te alimentes.

I'm Messed Up and that's Okay

I am tangled up and knotted
like the friendship bracelet
I never finished making.

In the midst of my unraveling
the world is hitching a ride
on the passenger side.

All that's left is:

>A tightrope to walk on.
>A jump rope to skip over.
>A hoop to jump through.

Unknot the bracelet.
Balance on the tightrope.
Skip the jump rope.
Leap through the hoop.

I ask myself,
>*Who said I had to?*

Life is not an instruction manual.
When it comes to the next step

I decide.

Land of the Free

You have killed me and covered it up
with years of dirty dealings, political schemes, and economic
destabilization.

So entitled,
you made me dig my own grave.

Here I stay and here I say,
there is no glory in the profession of oppression,
no stardust left behind,
and no ticket to heaven reserved
for those who ill-treat humankind.

Island Life Part I

My mind is an island.

    Unmoored.
        Vast.
            Isolated.

My mind is an island.

    Vibrant.
        Expansive.
            Wild.

My mind is an island.

    Savage.
        Unfiltered.
            Lush.

Island Life Part II

My mind is an island,
and its biodiversity astounds me.

Mountains and rivers, and rocks that lead into water falls
that ricochet into massive oceans.

My mind is an island, but it lacks
an oasis. I walk and swim for miles

looking for the promised land. My feet have yet to touch
a plane of existence in which I can rest in peace.

Though my mind is an island
it has not reached its final evolution.

Much like the laundry in the basket
in the corner of my room it is still very much in progress.

I set my sights on new horizons and commence
folding. Starting with my delicates.

Green(go) Invasion

You are a pest
slinking around this island.
Strutting through what you perceive
to be prime real-estate.
Camouflaged by viridian-green

you emerge from forgotten foliage.
Invader, you navigate this terrain
like the king of Spain. As if you own
this place.

No crown rests upon your head.
No royal blood courses through your
ectothermic veins.

Plague, you sprawl
across the land buying up sacred space. Peering from the highest
treetops
in search of the next flora and fauna you might displace.

To you we are all prey.

Iguana,
monocular-eyed beast,
scale-clothed monster, emblematic of the cobble-stoned streets
en el Viejo San Juan.

An invasive species you still remain.
You extend your claw-tipped hand and take.

Green, go!

We will follow the scientists' heed and make a meal
out of you. Place you over a spit, turning
for an even sear above crackling embers.
We will savor your taste with cheer
as you once scoured our home.

Maybe I'm Better off Broken

Sometimes I want to shatter
like ice beneath a sturdy set of molars.

Crushed.

Pulverized into a finite dusting of crystalline shards.
Shards that remain stuck
needling their way down your throat

Sometimes I feel like I'm melting
maybe I'm the condensation gathering on the rim of a glass
or drops of water that cling to grassy blades on dewy morning days.

Sometimes I'm a mime and can't self-actualize
pushing at the walls of my prison.

Wailing in silence and unable to spring myself free
like a Jack-in-the-box while onlookers point and jeer
from their top-notch seats.

Trapped.

On the bad days, I find myself oscillating between

       here
           and
               there.

When the inner critic comes out to play
it feels as if the dissonance is here to stay.

Residue

We are the dregs
floating miserably
at the bottom
of a coffee pot.

Listlessly,
swishing and wishing
someone would place us in their cup.

We languish

in our destiny
to be poured
down the drain.

And long
for something better
in vain.

Tsunami

lo que se atraviesa en mi camino.

y consumir con ferocidad

para arrasar con todo

Quisiera ser un tsunami,

Same Key, Different Lock

If you ever let me go
I'd be lying if I said I didn't care but then
I'd never think of you again.

You clearly didn't see me for all I am
and that's on you for being low key.
What a shame, it's on your end.

I guess I'm just too high key
thinking I could be
more than your friend.

Formica

Crawling around
my person.

This sensation creeping
and coating my dermis

like a candied apple
steeped in heated sugar.

Lacquered over
with a bright finish.

Impossible to efface.

I chipped my tooth
attempting to break skin.

I decided to tattoo it in.

Each pinprick,
a hiss, released
from demons
I won't miss.

Wearable, permanent art,
draped like finery.

Encircling ivy.
Embracing embroidery.

Akin to a canvas, broken
out of its frame, tired
of fitting in.

La Pala y el Rastrillo

No dejes que las raíces que has cosechado
toda tu vida impidan el crecimiento.

No te aferres
a lo cómodo, lo común, ni a la costumbre.

Que con el tiempo todo se desvanece.

El único constante es el cambio y no espera
hasta que te prepares para caerte encima.
Viene de la nada y deja todo pata arriba'.

El cambio como la corriente te arrastra
y aunque suele sonar desagradable
todavía le queda espacio a la posibilidad

para que le dé aliento al bien o al mal.
No se sabrá hasta que llegue lo sucedido
en el mismito instante.

Lo que queda es incertidumbre.

Pero, ¿quién dijo que el desconocimiento
no se podía disfrutar?

T.Q.M.

Some people might tell you that I say I love you too much.

Sometimes I think I don't say it enough. Like I'm afraid it might slip
like an acrobat vaulting towards impossible heights.

I love you
is an affirmation, a declaration. It says,
I'm here, you're here, us, and that's all that matters.
I say it often so that it won't erode

as time smooths out memory.
I love you is a reminder. It says, I see you,
I see all of you and I'm still here, we're still here, together.
I say it in different ways so it won't get boring.

I love you.
Te amo.
Te quiero.
Te quiero mucho, un montón.

I love you is a promise and an answer.
It's said with certainty and pleads for more time.
Te quiero mucho, un montón
treasures you and comforts me.

My I love yous grant me a sense of permanence which remains
unattainable. My I love yous tide me over
'til the next day. They say,

We will be here tomorrow.

And I get to say it all over again
with my whole chest.

Sana Sana

Mi isla del encanto,
¿Qué no me haz regalado?

Me baño en tus ríos y tus playas;
ahí mi espíritu recibe tu consuelo.

La etapa de renacer ha comenzado
y provoca en mí una paz interna.

Lloro abrazada en las faldas de tus montes y cuando llueve
el cielo se lleva las lágrimas derramadas.

Respiro el aire fresco, la briza me apapacha,
y hasta tu agua bendita me llena con una energía curativa.

Fluye como la corriente
brindándome la fuerza
para empezar de nuevo.

Patria

I may bleed
red, white, and blue,
but it doesn't have the same meaning for me
as it does for you.

Oasis in the Sky

I come from a place
where the oceans meet
the might of mythology.

I come from a place
bathed in golden light
and enchanted by canopies
of gracious green.

I come from a place
donde tendemos la ropa
and the breeze lends us stray gusts
of wind to help them dry.

I come from a place
where the people sing and sway:
—*Temporal, temporal,*
allá viene el temporal.

I come from a place
that has been swallowed
by the eye of hurricanes.

Consumed yet still alive.

I come from a place
with star-strewn skies.
Estrellas hung high
like candle lights.

Where to look up is to be aloft in space
an interstellar surprise.

Where the hand of the gods
has chosen you to ornament the night.

Alas

Como un colibrí
aprendiendo a volar
salté de mi nido sin saber
cómo iba a resultar.

Es por su bien,

dicen.

Le echamos veneno
a las flores,
dizque por su bien.

Le echamos veneno
y aplaudimos.

Gritamos:
—Crece, florece.
 Por favor, ¡crece fuerte!

Le echamos veneno
para después cortarlas
hasta el tallo
y ponerlas sobre la mesa.

Nos reunimos
para un velorio sin pena.

Un momento de silencio.
Es poco, ¿no?

A lo único que le rezamos
es a la cena.

Espero que te disfrutes
ese plato
de arroz con habichuelas.

In my Image

I'm not religious
but if God exists
she is a woman.

•••

When the universe birthed me
it built me out of flaws.

God wasn't afraid to bend a few laws on this one.

She reached her hand into a bag of tricks
and one by one pulled from sporadic traits

and like building blocks tossed together
I began to take shape.

She broke ground with a sledgehammer.
Left a few walls for me to demo.

Poured the cement that made up my foundation,
but left a couple cracks
for me to fill in.

She left plans for me to follow,
but one by one
I redrew the outline
so I no longer felt swallowed.

Heart's Afire

I am not slaying my dragon
I am making it my pet.

My sword is not a weapon meant for bloodshed,
but a tool to catch a glance at my own

reflection. My sword will not pierce a soul. My eyes will
do the piercing and reveal sights unseen
images which my mind may wish to keep.

My dragon will not remain chained up for eternity,
but will instead roam free exploring the dark skies
immensity.

My dragon is my fear personified:

> *My mind betraying me.*
> *I am meant to be alone.*
> *That I'm rotten to the core.*

Every roar grates my bones and crescendos
a pathway down my nervous system.

I refuse to carry it for my slender shoulders would cave
beneath its weight. I would rather let it soar.
To relieve my body of a soreness that reaches sinew.

The fire it releases will not seek to burn.

I will harness the flames and craft myself a set of wings
to take flight
high alongside the wind.

Alight; with a furnace in my chest
and sparks in my lungs. Unlike Icarus
I'll never get too close to the Sun.

Feelings Can Also Lie to Us

I can't breathe.

Your feet are at my throat,
stomping away
at the words I can't let out
       or is it in?

I can't remember
             anymore.

I can't breathe.

I choke on my success
it lodges itself
in my esophagus.

Success.
I was force fed it
never quite managed
to cough it up.

I can't breathe.

I look in the mirror
and see a smattering of paper cuts.
I use salt-water to seal-in the hurt.
A weight sits on my chest
and it refuses to get up.

It cracks my sternum.

To resuscitate myself,
first,   some things must be broken.

I can't breathe.

Expectations surround me.

No.

They lock me in,
corner me,
trap me,
suffocate me.

I don't know why I'm here.

I can't remember
                      anymore.

I can't breathe.

That's a lie. I'm a liar. That's all I do.
I breathe and I do it again and again
and I don't stop.

Can't stop.
Won't stop.

Because if I did
then I wouldn't
and I won't.

That's when it's over.

It's not over.

La Ortografía

Pal carajo con las reglas
de la ortografía. No aguanto
que ni una coma nos separe
de un suspiro al otro.

Salvaje

Quisiera ser un ramo
de flores silvestres.

Para sentirme como una pieza
fundamental de esta tierra campestre.

Esta lengua no se traba

Esta lengua
está llena
de rabia con ganas de soltarla
y no solaparla.

Antes que corten el hilo
donde el mundo está tendido.

Animado
como un pecho
apoyado en un sostén

y colgado en el infinito.

Sun-kissed

The sun's heat chases away the uncertainty
worming its way down my veins.

The uncertainty peers
over my shoulders on a day-to-day,
lying in wait, ready to prey.

Transforming my perception
into one of bated deception.

She'll taunt me for my lack of know-how.
That's what's got me so afraid

with doubts running a marathon up in my brain.
It's a challenge to stay sane.

I have to stand firm against this bane
unless I want it to be the source
of my unending pain.

I must let the clouds part,
let the chips fall where they may.

Replace uncertainty with wonder
let it take the reins.

Wepa

Yo soy mi propia victoria.

Words I practiced in the mirror,
but didn't believe.

At least, not yet.

Not a reflection of my current situation,
but something I wanted to project.

Take a wish and sculpt it.
Make it true.

My truth.

Let it take up space
as it should.
Yo soy mi propia victoria.

A phrase I wanted to shout from the rooftops,
and when I said it aloud,
I wanted it to taste
of blue and green Pop Rocks

exploding across my tongue

instead of a spoonful of cinnamon
that got stuck in my throat,
and left me choking.

I wanted to own that shit
and scream

—WEPAAAA

into the void.
And see,
what it would say back.

Porque yo soy boricua
y yo

no me quito.

Smile on me

The sun showers my face.

Where there once were blemishes
flowers sprout and take their place.

Pores open to breathe
in the possibility of what awaits.

Acknowledgements

I have been known to hand out my gratitude liberally to those who matter to me, but it seems I forget to save a little for myself. In trying to correct that bad habit, I want to give myself the thanks I deserve, for fighting, for writing, for healing, and for taking this risk in writing this book.

I want to thank my parents and my sisters for never giving up on me and always cheering for me. Without them I would not be here today, and I would not have been able to continue with this labor of love and pain.

I am more than happy to extend my thanks to Alegria Publishing, especially Davina Ferreira, who shares her heart with everybody and is successfully making community for Latines Artists where they are safe, seen, and supported. Davina, eres una mujer divina. You believed in me, and that's all I needed.

I wish to express the deepest gratitude to my fellow writers, who have been willing to listen to my works in progress and supported me every step of the way. Whenever I doubted myself you set me straight.

Thank you to my therapist. For your patience and teaching me how to save myself. I will remember to let the train pass through the station.

Le quiero dar las gracias a mi Tío, Olvilio Vazquetelles, quien cada vez que me veía, me señalaba y decía:

—Esa nena va a ser escritora.

And to the woman who made this reality an achievable goal, I give thanks to my first grade teacher, Mrs. Stout, from Saddlewood Elementary. You helped me learn how to find answers for the curiosity which lived within. I have never forgotten you, and will always hold you in high esteem.

Bio

Kamilah Mercedes Valentin Diaz is a chronic overthinker, who also happens to be publishing her debut poetry collection, *Morivivi: To have Died yet Lived*, with Alegria Publishing. Originally from Puerto Rico, Kamilah has tons of experience with change, but during the pandemic she was forced to sit still. With so much time to spare and her mental health circling the drain Kamilah began to write again. Her family, sheer stubbornness (she's a Tauro), therapy, and writing journey helped her come back to life. As a college senior attending Purdue University, Kamilah is ready to get back in the thick of it and hopes to attend grad school to achieve an MFA in Creative Writing.

KAMILAH

TO HAVE
DIED
YET
LIVED